The Bow

Mira Mattar

Published 2021 by the87press
The 87 Press LTD
87 Stonecot Hill
Sutton
Surrey
SM3 9HJ
www.the87press.co.uk

ISBN: 978-1-7399547-1-0
Cover art: Pauline van Mourik Broekman, *Untitled*, collage, 35.5cm x 27.5cm, 1991
Design: Stanislava Stoilova [www.sdesign.graphics]

Now I am not dissociated from my ululation. I hear the roaring and the roasting and know that it is I.
– Gillian Rose

Oh,
We who wanted to prepare the ground for friendship
Could not ourselves be friendly.
– Bertolt Brecht

...there are some who consider this way of seeing, which is to say, focussing intently on the most minor detail, like dust on the desk or fly shit on a painting, as the only way to arrive at the truth and the definitive proof of its existence.
– Adania Shibli

for friends

Contents

Minnows

i

It fails. Just as I learn how to love
it   my instrument, my hill alone
        a tulip a yellow embrace   I worked
as a shill for my enemies
  in the last days of their world.

Under a poison sky
I crouch   calculating negative pressure
newspaper crunched into planets burned
sucking the flesh into cups

small drama of Aprils arc inside
my running shift from from to to
  wanting made me
                at last needless   I was
not   a drained fluid tapped
byproduct discarded centuries of whey
        Mary, my stomach
my big bowel
            my linings   my bully   my moulds.
Unhinged by a swung open window
these greens   these greens   so sweet
                                so sweet.

The decision is constance itself
  un/making form
                              stretched taut on a hoop
   like every time I love you
      shines as a well in the chaos
like writing
  a surface
  pleasure/s a poem un/making time
                                  like every guy
at the autoshop weaving his voices through
blue railings so sweet
                                so sweet
              a single bed, Leamington Spa
I'd like to stop and suck their cocks for hours the galaxies
behind the eyelids darling
                                        keep walking lonesome   slip
the track into the gutter   never find me
        playing Minnie Riperton to the dill.

Leave me my hell alone
for at least 40 days of lack   caught
our pockets strained with coins at the arcade forbidden
   being eight   big mouths stuffed with ice cubes
giggling nectarines sliced up for sacrifice
                                                    the tribe   a plastic name

in my heartless heart of hearts
 I never found   no one so I could
see everyone
                draw my own face out of nothing, turn
 my own back out of love
wait   I want to lay you down come here
  I'd like to stroke your forehead
hey did I say I was sorry
come here I learned the word and –

ii

for L.

mornings I mistake
wanting some other world with wanting
just a fuck, a tender hand
inside the correction pressed upon the forehead
not in its pale and secret heart
wishing me smooth and placed
at an Easter table with the other eggs. I do
not resist but it will not do
or undo   a civil war, demolition, your mother,
bile duct cancer, capital, rape, dopamine imbalances
the suburbs or sickness –
it will not do or undo what was spat in my face
or what my face spat back.
Old journals
record minor devastations   piled
into major ones making
at least one tendon in one arm of the world/s
architecture   you should have seen
me   cockily storm the ocean
as if it was merely a lake
tapping the unlikeliest source   a row of teeth
a knife in a lime in Edenbridge Town
these greens, these greens so sweet
so sweet
I did resist
bedraggled car sick clawing the lid of murdered sky
I did resist
all the he's
glint inside the left brain tucked

behind an ear the shadow
forming by the communal bins is definitely not just a fox
walking backwards into tense and agile fingers
in the hallway telling me
what I am under the Italianate roses
of this indefensible Europe behind the eyelids
darling squatting with our goats at the passport office how
he loved to see me cry
you fuck
here's my tax receipt, here's us snuffling
for our chicken dinner
someone's always getting pushed
down the stairs unevenly here
or in Worcester Park, there or in a Bangladeshi
H&M factory the plughole of the Amathus Beach
Hotel was always gurgling with blood
I rested
inside this equation for a lifetime
but whichever way I balanced it I was dead
and so were you, and so were the cleaners
at the Amathus Beach Hotel.
At the little red table
D shuffled truth 'til I unfastened my grip
on waiting for conditions
and the symptoms of conditions to align
with laying down at 40
still hoping to be tucked in
the shadow leaks
from under the bed ready
to work you dead –
you're face down on the ground
everything tastes metallic
you turn your own mouth over in the dirt

iii

that was where they congealed, the men
crossing Darling Row
        me at 34 at 6 at 29 at 18 grey
blood siphoned out into their spines.
    I was so young, and ugly
as a baby bird
I shoved a child who had my face
into a textbook and ignored it.
      I fought a man to death on the Queensway
just for looking at me wrong.
                    I thought to stand beside
someone who knew would mean that I knew too
and that *that* knowing would keep me safe
and that I knew what *that* word meant a little or at all
or how it felt
or if I wanted it most or least of all
or if it was the same or opposite to leaving
   in the middle of the middle of the night
  medlar peel finer than paper
stripped in crescents of orange
  twist in your palm
like a fortune fish, like a tongue –
                                I don't want answers
I want escape.

iv

Sometimes what appears as friendship
is only violent agreement
    revealed as such when you step
unknowingly, out of line
having mistaken again
a walled garden for the world
        or having yourself suggested a universe
  instead of only a bilious fist.

Though I may not shake your hand in the end
I think I always want my fist to be opened
even if that means
        pressing a palm to the sky in farewell
even if that means falling down, letting it catch me,
snapping my wrist   even if it means
it's only me here
            with my paw against my brow.

I have no time anymore for force
disguised as passion disguised
again a scare   scooping detractors
  into the drain and filling it with vinegar and bicarb
in the name of purity   not every deviation
is betrayal   every blockage is not
        the final aneurysm
though it may appear sudden if your eyes've been
    closed to the drip and my mouth has never
a true word said.

Why sever this baby connection?
A little white bench covered in bird shit
dappled with California lilac.
Honey look at my pasta pot!
I remember our chests heaving in the doorway.
Lots of you live high up
we could see fireworks from Walworth
all across London
there is a zig-zag house   too well curated
just about big enough to hold everything down. I wanted
to argue that DIY is the opposite of sex,
and gardening is sex but enlightened, to joke
but I saw something ugly all at once
in you so inside me too.

Scale was frightening me again.
How righteous the arch of a foot I loved
pushing my head down
I like sleeping on my face! Nourishing
my devastation later
in a couple of drawings blind
is the one who makes friends easily
who forgets the ringing telephone is an option
not a command
moving towards moving towards –
I sweat like a giant
silent as a pin.

v

Unfortunately I remember everything.
Except when I have to ask again how to exhale
  every time, how to pump my tyres
what year the county was incorporated. Either
      I'm a doll, a darling, or difficult
to get along with   my unwillingness
  to abandon the time you didn't stick up for me
outside Euston station
  the cringing drizzle
  of England   the seep, the arrogance
    its flattery
sullen
  I wanted her to want me
and would sleep alone to prove it   a fly
                                                    flies in and out
                                        I lift two snails from the path
                                          three black cats stop and nod.
Fine you think I'm an idiot.
Still I won't deny the contradiction
      inside care
of self of other of slug
          a storm a wilderness, narrow –

I heard that everyone all along thought I was wrong
and a stupid jerk. Fine.
Smash your head and say I did it.
Be the angel nephew
    mouth full of bird food, fine.
I've been called worse.
                I won't answer the phone. Fine.
I'm the mad dog.
Shoot me in the head.

One kind word for every three unkind
won’t ease my hunger   won’t deny the daring of my size,
                                                                        I was getting bigger
down the steps at Surrey Quays
   shame in sonorous fret
                                            the click of my jaw, my hollow sandal
  I did resist
while we adored
    audacity in others
but shrank it in here
                              puff,
                             a lymph tapped and drained.
I ask for less and less I say less I wake up less I want less
shaken for being a boring toy
    curt,   a pet I totally agree.

I always was a pest
when I said I can't believe you ever loved me
pointed at the legal spiderweb
a love letter
telling me who started it
saying only the massiveset scaredy cat would be scared
of the friendliest wolf –
blood on my legs
my cheek red
head off on the overground.
I can't help being spooked every time
kindness is conflated with weakness
and sadism is disguised
as the maverick voice of truth,
this is the voice that wants only itself
this is the chicken
at the kitchen table baby
I made your favourite
why'd you always ruin everything? Oh
these undercurrent glances
drip into the lungs year by year.
Crisp summer mornings
when you hated me most –

fresh shadows sharp as collar,
pulse of a ceiling fan thrum
peaches, hot fries, my sinuses glassy and salted.

I was so young, and ugly
as a baby bird.
I had a tube attached to me. My thoughts could not
gain entry.

I left so many cities
with my stupid ugly wheelie suitcase,
Costa Earl Grey burning through the padded maroon cup
half a flapjack sweating in my pocket.

I fall into the pile of glass again doctor again
before I remember everything
    on the edge of bed
  on the top of the hill
    my mind in one hand
  the wall in the other.

These are the things   I used to feel
that sometimes return like remembering
  learning language.
I love to hear the hollow form
inside the lines. I decided the shape of my fs
                                        the loop
                                     the noose
                                       the bow
                                    infinity.

vi

Viscid crown
sunk city skyline
sucked up like flesh into cups.

I dream of wasps and trying
to count
all these white tulips,
buttery and hale.

What? I like Nature
too, its torque
the unfolding

in Croydon we pull from
the dells every stamen
and garland the skirts into wreaths

not yet cognizant of time,
that silver anxiety
Silk Cut coloured   time will tell
that is God will
that is time will
God willing

my remedy is metal
my friends are violet weeds

I watch from my third womb.

How can we do anything with anyone?
Every group assaults itself
and is ringed with managers.

Every unending back
I almost drowned in
loving every water
costume always in my bag.

In that cold river I saw
minnows and mud
and swans from underneath –

vii

low orange moon
full over the estuary
a can, a smoke
lightly entwined
an adult knows it must not destroy.
Things are in the oven.
Stuff is in the veins,
the head is on the top now look
what you made me do. Yolk again
orange too
another glossy morning
I get to be a shadow
vaguely that weapon
keeps us/e in the zone
of always looking over our shoulder
vigilant clambers a blade-
black dahlia cuts a river in space
as it falls
thick point drags
us ankle bruised from ocean watching
swifts for hours dip
you never took a single photo of
me vain pup suckling tick
check you really love me
every day until you don't –
I'm too slick a mirror really
magnifying every crater I'm abyssal babe relax
the air is pretty I've taken
you out enough times haven't I
built your Character for free
a dangling novelty
if to live you need to think the river isn't running to the sea

my veins don't end in me
an apoplectic chunk
a cadmium red
unpicking the difference
between a rhythm and a loop –

vii

for E.

I have eaten enough ice cream on both sides
  of the other woman's other woman
enough times to know I do not know   completely
the androgyny of an iridescent face
      how it angles
light's colours
                      splits
                                     contains all
      follicles singed
                                                   helixes
scraping mould off a vortex
                                                     head tilted back
                                 enough times
      all our eyes
 at the sight of all our mothers
  and all our mothers' eyes
enough times
at the sight of all of theirs   have curled
                                      inwards   forever   strategising exits –

when   I meet the paramour's mother
the best friend's
metallic bug   stunned inside her crystal hair
wings' hinge rusted
on the trail
of night buses home from Hackney after half-fucking
someone else's someone at the edge
of a pulsing blue   bedroom I have quaked
and hidden   my fat thighs enough times
I have been both sides of oh you're
cousin daughter girlfriend slut upstairs
at the Funky Munky patent white Mary Janes all day
I watched a rose
unfurl today like all roses its bloom looks exhausted
I was a nipple under the sink
sliding my hand for the baggie
here   I've only only just started
the spoon is half-way out her mouth I'm bleeding
hot yellow towel round my neck
wet hair fills the tubes
my little red table
waits for you all
you who turn the cards and smirk
because you have what I want or want what I have
or know what I want and will never have
though now
I am needless as spring –

fuck
my brain is expanding outside Bank tube
a hand is on my throat
in a beer garden in Finsbury Park
another is sliding up my leg
if he ladders my mum's low deniers I've really had it
    bruising my hair with his fat
Christmas fingers
            he's telling me how I feel
all the things I'm capable of
        how I seem fairly intelligent
can I speak the other/s language
can I say some dirty words   baby
                            I whisper
the recipe to the Molotovs my father threw
    I am an improvised incendiary weapon
I knee him in the face with the back of my elbow
I lick my brass knuckles as he goes down
                            this is my only heirloom
he squats cursed in the gutter
looking for his coke
searching his cavities like a cop
    I rub the drain cover into my skin for proof –
this is S's pretty dress
this is not what binds or unbinds us.

You are a shimmering baby
blue field of irises.

You in your pink poloneck, brown suede jacket
you in the white Barry M eyeliner
you, the kind one
I am twice your size and don't know how to stop it
    if I fuck him quietly in your spare room

maybe I'll stop wanting your herb garden
    and immaculate waist

I am very unraveling
under a sick spring sky
I crossed so many bridges
Lambeth Palace, Westminster Abbey, The Tower
runs the city blood
down my legs
I'm a fat pigeon fighting
a shrinking
come round
I like your drawings is all
how there's no background to hold the objects
but they don't look like they're floating
I don't need to feel like I don't exist. You know
I alone am getting older
stop rubbing it in   your eternal breast
keeps reduplicating under 30
girls keep getting born.

Look, my daddy never combed my hair
my mummies made theirs subtle and white
arranged me backwards into the sink pretty
        as a formula
I cry
I learned this alone
                                I said for years
   but you were there too casually
emboldened by mid-morning baths
by audibly rolling your eyes
by refusing to be taken as a shield –
      you're like
how clear day after clear day after clear day clouds
                                                                are spectacular.

viii

Glass and baby gro winter
not a cloud in the sky of it, very hygienic
streakless a hexagon falling
shattered inside her thighs. We lay on her bed
and she let me
follow the scar/s silver time
in a sparrow trail
caught in the trim

woodpecker, a great big spider, my great big brain
single use latex
gloves peel off   pedal bin step swing clang
forty orchids garlic minced
browsing at the silicones, Chick Pea I love no king.

A row of golden animals marching
on a belt. I was a baby gossiping
with L drinking coffee, smoking   layers of winter,
glass, blood in a pool
I splinter
sheen   I am cast as the mirror
saving my little seeds.

I don't know what I am and I like it like that
I don't know who I will love
or what they may call themselves
Chick Pea from the palm
at the end of my mind
I don't know who I will love.

A shape in light appears on the wall, goes
        then appears then goes
you note it's the score of your movements
block/unblocking a sunbeam
                        patch in a flash like minnows.

Sleeping With The Window Open

That gulf again
I am a raw egg rolling towards its incredible mouth
indelible the chasm that ends language
I clutch the sides of the kitchen my hands dissolve
the floor goes my stomach exits
you are not my friends
having never considered a thing from a severed head
hanging out the window
having never had to consider impalement
having never scoured under the bed scooping an arc
with your skull
sifting the earth for clues a signal laying with foxes
kicking in metal bins so every time you pass
you know at least that dent is you
me I took what I didn't have and placed it between
the aluminium organs not knowing it at all
or what it would render inverted on the backs of my eyeballs
in the middle of the middle of the night
I had thought casting it out was a kind of safety
but it burnt my oesophagus
on its way back up having never left
none of this means I want it
or do not want it
it's there
and so am I
sure sometimes I hear voices
this doesn't scare me
I don't need to know which is mine
when I was small this hurt me
always searching getting my fingers shredded
by a tin can I was trying to use as a telephone

always distracted
if I could only just then finally I'd
no verb no noun no going no home
I know some of you feel it too   under under your t-shirts
like catching sight of your reflection
when you didn't mean to be looking
curved distorting over a car window
swirling in oil iridescent
in the mirrored glaze of the city   in its smashed glass
suddenly   excluding nothing
there you are
reflecting the burning sky –

I betrayed myself   all the way to Sarah Jane's
peeked into the eyes of her mother's golden dog
and saw the bombastic confidence of owning her
of ownership   of naming
I laid my hand upon her head
and asked for a non betrayal
of non self that wouldn't resolve in pride
or sameness   or high definition   or edginess
or jamming the cream whip to the back
of the throat and inhaling
or stuffing your head deep in the honeysuckle and
getting it stung   raw
or getting full from somebody else's hunger
or getting big from this war
tell me who is the psychopath
your parents eat pizza with utensils
brother I know your country
your eyes in the rearview mirror
the god inside your chest
I dunk my head inside the chemical

I know we cannot touch   suffering   English desserts
I was concave with wanting Annabel
if Annabel meant white toast at a wooden table
set honey   soft butter
laughter   a dead pig on Sundays
if Annabel meant being in the world without a viscose
film around you   pressing your fingers to
but never piercing
lapsed   a lurching gait
I strip off my nightie   plunge it into acid
I sleep in my uniform   one eye open I hound the fetid ghosts
tell me from the neighbour's biscuit tin
what were you doing there and why
did you know my grandfather
how sweet were the apricots
and what was the scent of the velvet light
I know what you did to the roaming dogs
I know how you got
the women in your house
someone will fall from the window
someone else will jump
an insomniac will scrape yellow melon seeds
out like brains into the rubbish
undulating in the sea of people killed crossing it
the name of the three year old Syrian Kurd was Alan Kurdi
but more will remember Ai Weiwei's
speak for yourself
art is beauty
I don't want to know any more
about this uninhabitable world
about every failed circumvention
every stone thrown
the football is on
the meat is being reheated safely until

three women
a Ghanaian an Indian and a Palestinian walk into
a Buddhist centre
agreeing on starches diverging on fats
who is the stand up immigrant
recruiting collusion
who keeps their neck for standing on yours
is the same eager trade as counting on
your suffering to unfold
in an antiseptic chamber then killing for it
I needed a joke
this lot fear a grain of rice
being in a car with you
the clingfilm sliding off let's go faster
I am completely alone
he she it is completely alone
smile
here comes little Timmy to call you that word grab him
push him down kick his face
oh I wanted to but
we were told the police were the solution
to a problem like this my edges were a blur
I was learning that the world re/solves
problems by naming and hiding them
just outside the zones called civilised
sealing them behind
a heavy metal seam
to mark what is not like you
what you need for your you-ness
I couldn't tell when my skin met anything
so I couldn't hear it when she said that in the kitchen
through the dazzling snowfall of August
fresh baguettes French lavender
that it wasn't that she didn't like me

it's that she could only do it from above me   forcing
me to crack my neck
hey
I can spit sideways   right into the wind of your lovability
then I went
to who was defined   to who walked boldly in and out
of rooms   conversations   traffic   universities
restaurants   swinging their attributes   spreading
their influence
I went and I knelt and I wept and I begged
at the feet of forced participation
never told a name in my summer diary
every day was one of my hundreds of cousins
erased   protected   my ugly heart
where is my agent where is my prize
where are my murdered brothers
I'll never surrender
their names
I'm always one side of betrayal
a dripping tap
against my ribs   it drags and clangs against the city's
prohibitions electric   nailed to public squares
the iron sound rings out
the sickly London twilight freezes another man dead
you need the abandoned as much as it needs you
nothing needs me to do anything
but shut the fuck up   is what was made clear to me in
love letters
and institutional communications   I get to sit here
with my own email address
sniffing pissy ankles
for a shit day rate or the swindle called experience
or power in a blinding strike   this shirking echo
was never what I thought our phantom dream was for

as long as I
shut the fuck up   everywhere   from Stansted Airport
to the fashionable office
to my own poetry reading   to mutual acquaintances
so I found the histories of
tongues cut out   and I found the histories of the cutters
and like you I was angry and in pain
but still wanted the possibility
of my whole heart
and wanted you to want yours too
and I learned my power   and I learned yours
Annabel
and I see it now   all at once
inside how much I hated being what I was in front of you
and how much you needed me to hate it
Annabel
you loved me for it.

I am only the proofreader on her haunches
squatting   somewhere with official gardens
snuffling at the golden trough
a statue urinating triumphant arcs of blood
between the folded thighs   tweaking the grammar
I long to recover from
wanting to hurt what hurts me
or is that the trick we labour
at the threshold of
and what if what hurt me
is also me
and what if I hurt it back
and what if it twists time into the trailing vortex drag of wanting
to get better
when what I need is to get bad enough

to locate the permanent tunnel
but every time you think you've found someones to do it
or not do it with
the layers peel back
to show sadism fossilised in a
predictable skeleton at its core hungry for bones
doubling as telescopic truncheons
you're told were found between your chilblained
fingers
so scared of seeming wanting
that you turned on need completely
oh saint
who will clean up your sacrificed self
doc I'm after the root
tell me what's inside me
I'm only a baby clutching my machines to my breast
for pillows again
help doc
I need a diagnosis is where did I begin officer
I know too much has been made of origins
but I know I didn't decide these names
or I wouldn't be stretching around with words
half pacific
sullen not sorry at all
here I can stomach the terrible fact
the men who kill
also sweetly burp their babies in the sunless winter
yes this is a lullaby
scrambling my simple dog heart
I was seeking the bridge
my hand was open
a tulip
my fingers were jabbing upwards as if into an opponent's eyes
the edges of my mind

what am I supposed to be compassionate limitlessly?
Where else could we point ourselves?
the only logical opposite is licking
your own shit off your own tail forever –
vengeance describes so many borders
what does my great hate do to me?
You're right I'm behaving 'like a woman'
a tick on a handsome leg
you're right I'm a footnote
if I'm even cited
what does your great hate do to you?
Where does all that loving go?
Tell me little language
I am really asking
the neon rose dead for two years
wanting you outside Sydenham Lidl
terribly
I am a wolf outside Triple M fried chicken
strapped outside my own initials
placing the pencils singly in their crunchy tray
clicking the tin shut
was the only sound I could make
repeating the sound repeating the question
tell me little language must I love him too?
Your definition of love can be
big enough to do what you must
yes
for this is the love encompassing all
our meticulous fury
all our creamy avalanches
terribly I am a wolf
repeating the question
What shall we do with this separate girl?
The folding urge envelops deviation

must be quashed   or locked away   or held
                    splayed   within the catalogue
                                its tissuey cradle
and labelled what are you complaining about?
                         An exhibit ornate and meaty
you may not be lost to the real beyond
                       to a future of your making
   where you might turn your back
        and in the turn's breeze reorganise the air
   sharpen its pellets
into a kind of acid
                    the folding urge absolves the folder
birthing fairness again
                      why are you always fighting it?
stay to the right of me you say
you will slip me a flower pressed
   you will slip me a filigreed angel
you will slip me a permanent invitation
                     so when in the centre of evening
I jolt choking and damp
I cannot point to you and say you did anything
   other than welcome me
        you need me to prove you
clean   and harmless
Ach! Leave me
        to my particular route
the only way to solitude with everyone at once
with every gnat with moss
                          there are so many ways to touch
in the dark –

        ach! My mind's always sinking and flying
I'll be back in a week or two

you need something beside you
a vision
without revenge
I have closed all my tabs
I am going swimming
all I want between us is an edge now
but that's your problem
how else to know what names us
granules in a coffee cup
at Mama's kitchen table   that alien IKEA white
what is this material   cardamon?
No
we are a modern people now   with modern furnishings
the old town is an intoxicating mix of traditional and new
ancient and high tech
everything left out   is everything I save
vagrant heart
going through the rubbish   golden   containing
traces of everything
you need   to start anew   rot and ruin   shattered
wing mirror
image shattered in it
this immediate air
we take what we need
we give it to each other
a bag of spring greens on New Cross Road
working it out backwards
food is just ingredients
demystifying innocence guilt suffering unleashed
wreaked equated
as though there was one doer behind one deed
calling itself a me
and standing behind itself
punishably

                    forgivably
    as though the water inside
is not the water out
                as though the gases the solids
began or ended in you
    as though a harmless life was possible
but you needn't kill the maggots to save the festering dog
              the judge punches out of the chest
enforcing itself
as though justice were a thing to inflict upon
a who becomes a what
is exploitable defined as such
    a what
        can think can love can fight
    if only in the heart inside the heart inside its heart
is bright
don't deny it
this is what comes to say
    words are not my   only   friends
no not diagnosing
    a what unmakes what made a what
like you is sleeping with the window open
            breeze like honey and butter on toast salty
        making the sweetness pop
no not diagnosing
    a what unmakes what made a what like you
is not mistaking what has marked it for itself
unguarded scar the path is clear
– a knife under the pillow
and nothing to defend.

Poem (29 December 2020)

after Bernadette Mayer

They thought one way of getting even was getting
rich.
I was looking up at the plastic wax rolling down
the candles knotted in the colonnade
with its imitation crystals bending imitation light   it was
mishung slightly off the ceiling's centre
and when I gasped and pointed at the lie
the grown ups said look here
is a photograph of Cousin Five dressed
as a British army general dressed
as a Jordanian army general dressed
as an Arabist come to pitch and pacify
nascent nation Glubb Pasha jaw undone
badged and bereted masquerade churning
consolation from exchange   guzzling outpost in the folds
of massacred maps   me
I'm here to study what studies.

Here is a leaky mirage on the edge of a bargain
stricken
at two empires' fault lines
rioting for daily bread in a squalling April subsidy
milled on the slip of protest quashed
easily from a magic circle   the skin is clutched
oh little egret
migrant passing over
have you seen in flashes what unseats

might also free
the path of bread from hunger   why cannot
I lift my limbs   why cannot I breathe big breaths
I have laid this feast upon my slothful unwed infants
these tourists   dollars strictly pegged
these fruits from the other side
there is a boulder upon my chest
is this inimitable hospitality all we have left
to serve is not the nature of any kind of people
please sit we have tea with mint
please our libraries are burning
you're right
what have we ever given the world only
a theory of light –

itself erased you chart and measure
the qanun's woven trail
every resonant note evades the ruler poised sword
raised   oh Bedouin, oh Circassian   child
when you turn from my country
you turn from me   you turn from yourself
learning nothing
yet you call yourself a lover
a scholar   a studious nun
this is not intelligence
between you and what bore you
between us and our formal and informal
enemies and friends   and by be/friend I mean leave gaps
between the notes
and hollows   tuck a fugitive rose   a bomb
a clue
on how to never be good again
my goodness take a walk with me

I'll drown you in the moss green river
the guilt oh Jesus
a silt deposit upon a velvet tongue
neurotic to call it politics
when by politics I mean
get the hell out of my bedroom
I mean it happens in the ruptures
I mean I want a world that does not drive you
to the final convulsion
your toes fitting smally inside the chainlink diamonds
at the top of the car park
at the top of the hospital
was that your final feeling   torpid
or was it falling?

Minor details grab and release us in the empty aisles
of empty vegetables like
was she wearing shoes or was she barefoot
was she in a patterned gown
polyester as summer uniform
or her own clothes   and if so which
and what happened to the clock I liked
Rick from *The Young Ones* on *University Challenge*
a P in front of the R swift
and vile a comedy puncturing not grief but its weight
leaving its edges
refined and wrought
a Byzantine confessional I see
a kind of filigree dappling my toes in the water every day
thousands of people die every week I cut
my nails into the shapes of his before showering
he kneels to eat my cunt
I lean to double the bath mat over
for his bones
and cup his mosaicked dome of skull
re-cut my nails into a shape
I can't remember through
as though shapes were not eternal
I am careful not to call them mine
fractious and lonesome
an oval   a square   a sensuous vault
the great octagonal steeple of my golden fingers
I never want   us   to be only what   he   they   is   are   not
or only what   I   you   am   are
or only what was left behind or out or on the side
or later baby
or an afterthought or an underthought when the thought is
split eviscerate hiss and fizzle
cigarette seethe in the hot summer gutter hey

I am the only one who loves you like   I do
and there's no lie in that I can point to   I am
a gullible girl and meaty
my head is tilted softly lit and lilting
I am still   too impressed by mercury   doesn't spill
or shatter but rolls in polished spheres spinning
on the kitchen tiles each maintaining its axial separateness
as well as it membership to being
mercury   that measuring element a baby's mouth full
of bubbles shining
fine as ferns
and shimmering   winter ink
tell me how I feel the weather
the pressure of my blood its pleasure   plug these sugar-rotted
holes of teeth   tell me again
you are the only one
who loves me like you do   silver tongued
and mobile quick
I was always a few steps behind
trying to communicate my exile
in my exiler's tongue
trying to point out a crow, a stream of piss
a sudden splash of the visible spectrum
blunt this magic thing I see
but cannot know   Mercury in my Third House says
I'm interested in reading and teaching, gossip and the daily news
I'm interested in whether it's erroneous to mistake
whatever you love for whatever you are
or whether this is only error when
whatever you love's a reflection without a shadow   me I love
the shadow's shadow uncleansable
I never want them
to be solely what they have done
in the mirrored arcade

a concertina crushed and wheezing
M says I like to get to the root
but fearing my power I tend to deflect
stray
ash
errant on the breeze.

My father's tooth fell out yesterday when he was eating a date.
I'd call this material for a joke about Palestinians
but I'd only have him to tell it to
I'd call this material for a rhyming couplet
date and forty eight
but satisfaction would distract you from the truth
the dates were old   his tooth was older
a rootless grotesque of silver-yellow bumps
a chunk unlike the tooth of the mind white
a diagram two neat roots like fangs themselves
concealed beneath the pillowy gum
pink as the ideal nipple I turned my back against
finding again purely taxonomy
the trade, the fix   to point, to claim   the stars
this whorling galaxy of hair   your birth
a speechless infant   I am the wet spring blossom
drifting with intent
towards the cool depth of the wreck
not knowing
what to call the state
that is the range
that is no longer looking up from under ground
but diving out of paradise   that super-mall hopping west
there is no future so there is no fear
to stop my motion
to stop my fingers trailing
in the open water.

Mama says it's itchy because it's healing
and I learned to start with the wound
but not to stick to it   a kind of anchor
which does not make me
an impossible creature
on the apple studded balcony elderberry bruised
and studying the corrugated plastic roof
pierced with burns from next door's cigarettes
through which it rains into our summer dinner
bowled in half-shells of grenades
mined and pinned domestic spread the terror   of my fingers
are in your mouth
and you are sucking every woman who ever
disobeyed you out of my unlimited capacity
for cold weather   my impression of a girl
hardy and British
and when you leave me I'm my own guest
strained and dripping through muslin
until I'm solid again and warm and oily and heavy
in my own bed today still everywhere is pain
being taken first for being alive and next
for winning an argument you were only having
in your head or online or in the mucousy cord
connecting the two   the unsolved spectre
in communion with all the terrible things
that happened all those years ago
or all the terrible things
that are happening right now
outside your window and far away
and in the space between you and the others
between your rib and rib
hungry ghosts scanned dry
thumb congeals in its joint   wrists crack
as the tragedy of reading feeds

the tragedy of conversation
seeking nothing but confirmation
calcifying the mellow throb of really thinking
gets hung, drawn, quartered at the crossroads
of doing nothing at all.
Look
I don't want to keep looking
for all the ways I'm bound
to get found out
for all the ways I've lost or am lost
or losing to all the things you
could call vampiric
to all the things
that have tapped into the animal
nodules of our brain folds weeping
under the bed, waiting
at the bottom of a staircase, trapped
and banging on the window, you shit,
a human, a mammal, a fool,
an irrelevant person with a bad body
and dull thoughts   a person
whose fault it is whatever it is
giving its real life heart beat alone
to what extracts the elements
of running the machine
I am writing on from the hands
of children in the DRC
and I can't stop thinking yeah I get why she did it
but why didn't I do more to stop it?
Guilt's purpose is to freeze you into a stationary
point around which a circle circles
making every attempt at escape into a kind of betrayal
a crime against the common and the dead
making nothing but itself

and you in turn
masking the face
of capital killer so good
we can either be surveilled or be alone
a failure failing   I need your touch
I need your lips upon my brow
this is not absolution
holding the red rubber heart
under the fog of river look
you are making something happen
with your personality alone
the bow around the scar we call ourselves
is detailing its every pleasure out loud
for it is incomplete if it is not witnessed
or celebrating a head severed
from which a new one grows spitting
deadly acid called shoot them in the legs
then have the gall to call us infidels
and normalise the handcuffed wrists of infants
painted blind with friendly insects this day is rags
this day is utterly sunless and I love so many people.
This day is soft lead.

I perfect my failing with you every year
and call it love
soon we will be 73 and my heels are metal
who would want their pleasure to ever be complete
I follow the motion
I move with it, I make it
I am an object of commerce
I am a subject of the century's steal
oh to be of the conversation
no one is trying to win

yes unfortunately I love
some who cannot talk without the joust
without the helm, the lance, the harness
those who scan and hunt and stalk
for fool or fault
and yes I call the opposite poetry
I stir the eggs I fall in love
here is the space for contradiction
to forge intelligence into joy
and yes I am re-constellating
the things that I am sure of
are not mine to wield
I lay down my love, I lay
down my mother, I lay
down my friends
I cannot explain why
I closed the door
without saying I wasn't ever coming back
I sensed the bind
was only sticky   that anything
I said would be used as ammunition
in the trial of being friendly
so I became what you would call a thing
between a coward and a bitch
a pussy and a cow
silently doing the opposite
but never without you all
sweet lilac plume the smog is red the birds
are disappearing
this day is bone-achingly cold
and I almost want someone to sleep beside
now that I'm feeling big –
oh, love
dilute me.

The cat comes down and we need to eat.
I touch her and my fingertips vanish into her winter fur
its undercoat of verdigris   her amber scent an amulet
a cinnamon biscuit outside Norwich station
a world ago March 5th 2020 I had missed the train to Yarmouth
where I met new friends for poems
for the ocean
for how to hew this death into a swirling murmuration
fruit and open country   we sever the sin
that ties us only to survival
and this severance saves us.
I'd been so unhappy
sitting on my little step absorbing
all my wrongnesses
and the fact that joy was gone all gone a baby puff
an edge   an asphalt pond
I stood up and called it arrival, called it maturity
called it politics
but still I was so hungry
so named my hunger greed
like you did
weightless white   called me lazy
for moving slow
I was an otiose foreigner confessing
into the thimble I am lucky to have
my thimble
my protected pushing finger oh
am I meant to be grateful for this glorious island
oh saint   not wanting hurts you just as much
as wanting does
my dusk, my lavender   who is my pleasure
dismembering now is the food
in my mouth somebody else's hunger yes
it is this order it is this murder it is this heat

it is inside us
I am a dying star, a deer, the seed inside an apple
swallowed whole, a shining pip
see the red ocean
see the green haze   see the black rain
blood and bile and tar
the boiling earth the server farm
thick tectonic hazard   we choke we open
our throats to sing
what is a song and what can it do
the poet's a threat to the state   the journalist
is murdered in the consulate
what is this dancing and who are these friends
that truly I would die without and for
what can I tell you
what can I see from this window
why do I miss you
I think of you packing your groceries
I try to remember spring –
who is my arrogant hunger feeding
this is your mother speaking
what are you working so hard for
who are you to think
everything on earth
is not already bending
towards the sun?

I prop the window open with a book
sleep all morning if you can, the sky spills
tangerine and coral.
Taupe-ish geese honk over
foxes ravage bin-fall
black cats arch and stalk the chipped steel fences
pinhole image shows an almost
infinite depth of field
where everything's in focus you must first
bear what you see
and then bear what you want
and then want it daily   a beam, a burst
a flash
a ray, a shaft, a blaze.
That was the last time in a long time
the windows blushed with threat of feeling
we were not taught how
this wilderness, this cityscape   I duck and dive
I squint   I get the wave of it
I know who decides whose violence is violent
I know not to trust anyone who says trust me
and insists
a hole in the cartoon forest
covered with a net of leaves
you idly spot a bird
pull from the earth a worm
and fall again and find it feels familiar
to be suspended in a pit
a kind of comfort
a secret language as I slip
another disc
just by sitting on a sofa
at some point you have to ask
is it me then or what?

Look, you can only blame
the mode of re/production
so far
and now you can think of something else
for the first time in your life your brain is yours
the communal jar, a gadfly
a lovelorn shearling
not yet tanned with chestnut, oak or sumac
oh odoriferous labour relegated to the edge of town
under the bridge
and over the hills
this whole area was forest from Croydon in the south
to Camberwell in the north
it was the Great North Wood
where I started receiving my memories
terrible birds
where I began the only work
is the work of the heart.

Or did I dream of her, the feeling of her
hands
or the feeling of missing her or of not
a silicone ribbon, a pulsing gateway
into all of us who are any kind of daughter
a condition impossible to be alone in
it was damp between my first breasts
again in L's pyjamas small
as a wet chicken
in the kitchen sink the red stockings
a palm
I never knew the ancient Levant's human statues
a string of lights she gave me
such warm pyjamas
cheap and slippery a not at all silken commodity
costly here in a mall in the west of the capital
we enter under metal the women
release their handbags to the scan
I am not the right girl-ish again
and everyone can see
I try not to abandon this flesh or stuff
or starve or hold it stiff or dear
I weave a rill between the factions
every girl or thereabouts I know's
too tired to sleep at night
with J and J outside the corner shop
where Stanstead Road and Brockley Rise
cross and touch
that dark green house
the dark green rivers below
The Peck, The Neckinger, The Effra
I excavated downwards
deciding
to be from here   a river

running hidden
to the water of the world
in my errant tenancy on earth
I learned that every
thing's more interesting than me
when I could stand / beside / myself at last
a silver egg inhaling through
a thawing surface streaked
in cosmic fuchsia
silk meat veined with emeralds trilling
at the milky crossroads dull
in Lewisham orange lit
the colour of insomnia.

We were drinking beers and talking
of the borough's borders and the smell
of depilatory cream and crème bleach
and scented sanitary towels
and the scent of unscented ones
and scented toilet paper
and dousing your cunt in live yoghurt
and '70s performance art
and the underworld
and siblings
when I was struck to one side recalling
how badly I cook when I'm hating
and how good it tastes when I'm with love
and how love's a state of remembering
everything
which when it's true has no opposite at all
an attention grows a focus sculpting
form not into being
but out of it

soft whipped peaks you hold the bowl
over your head and nothing collapses
you are not shattered
you are not a vapour
every time someone tried to tell me what I was
I learned more about them
than I did about me
as though there were only two options
disintegration or assimilation
eat or be eaten
Bernadette writes of chopping a carrot
how it seems to be returning to itself as seed
how when you try to hold down
anything you slip
and I will slip you
I want the agile particular
which isn't against the word
for together
don't you get it
this is my first and half language
my forked tongue
I am the colour of the sun
I am a humming bird
my sound is from my movement
not my song
is for my heart
I know torpor as a kind of rest
people are dropping dead even more Mama
is inside me now in the morning especially she is careful
in her motions opening the blinds, making coffee
taking the pin to her lashes
to separate them after mascara
a pin to the eye
trying always to see that's me

bothering the adults with my questions   even the doctor
when I asked if my do-nothing strategy
was a prodigious and Zen kind of healing
or whether I was cruel avoidant and a coward
suspicious and staid
scratched her head
if there is a storm
I will throw myself in it
I know the centre is still
am I a fool an eye   and if so which
my guts are stringy and compulsive I don't eat
in the mornings, I don't listen to voicemails
I am hale and crowing
in lime pools of ring-road traffic
trying to find a way to stop running
myself over
to stop turning myself in for just being
disagreeing, a horrible girl with a horrible face
and horrible thoughts in the end
I don't want to do much
but be lazy   unoccupied   to look at the free sky
and do nothing
so I'll go where I need to go
and do what I need to do
without being tracked without tracking myself
I can find where I began
the root of the word
but never its every nutrient
impossible to trace
an origin completely
is a task that can obsess you
admit it.

Elision's root is striking
as in hitting or pushing out
like big mushrooms low on trees
in signs of secret heart rot part
of me wanted her to strike out and be free
I'd knock on the window
so she'd look back and wave
and I'd know again
that she would live forever
but elision's root is crossing out
a pencil line through words
a vowel omitted
try for once to listen
to everything including you
king of the babies, thick electrical hum, pop
of dirt on seed, aural smudge
of cars imagined as an ocean,
breath, the pipes, the tinnitus screech, cat,
a whirring grate, Mr Horror's warden club,
the boss's clicking pen, rain
and a sound like a can
of paint being shaken
when I was very young
and saw those words about you
in the alleyway to school
and returned to paint them over
over your name's my name too
I hid it and the words
that followed and I hid my terror
and I hid the can
and I hid what I saw
and I hid what I did
and I hid how I felt
and was this strategic elision or was this

shame and did it stick and burn
inside my inside sun
and did it catch my tongue
and did it tear it out
and did I learn then how to only
write in truth and speak in lies
and did this make me a moving target for men
who like girls who can barely speak
whose dreams even are silent
though I often wake with words
a spell, a hex, a curse, a koan
sticks with me all day or longer
like when Emily writes
'I have dreamt in my life dreams
that have stayed with me ever after
and changed my ideas,
they have gone through and through me
like wine through water and
altered the colour of my mind'
I think of Audre's white margarine
kneaded yellow
and the yes bursts into me too I am swimming
under water Mama I heard the world
from inside you
for half a decade I didn't dream
and before then all I had
was mirrored cabinets
opening into nightmare arcadias
I would wake clutching the sweat-damp
angel hairs of European babies
pink-cheeked emblazoned
in tiny fantasias on touristy pill boxes
kitsch and hinging
open in rows

of mercury filled aunties' teeth glinting
with uterine solutions to unpleasant feelings
the injunction to embrace them concerns me
I mean I get it I do it
but I am not so conflict averse
as the brain questionnaires put it
that I don't know that part of an embrace
isn't also a tussle
isn't also slick and leathery
a dying tree
a young woman
recognises the folly of withdrawal
and grows larger reading under cover
to the unpleasant feelings well
I don't know about you
but the unpleasant feelings
have more than once embraced me back
saying they are pleasant ones
and know what's best
for stroking my scalp with their fingernails
tickling my deepest organs
is there green anywhere inside
besides in what's trying to exit
the ivy thrusts in through the vents
while we sleep below the canopy
I saw the umbra and its trick
there was no best as there was no god
as there was no motherless mother
and I saw how I had grafted and degraded
all my guests and only then
did I begin to know
when I was moving.

Like I said
I learn more about you
when you tell me what I am
than I ever do about myself big butterfly
catcher, wing-stretching servant of chauvinism
I have noticed this impulse for collecting
people and other creatures
this accessorising urge an explorer's
requirement to cross from a list
to hang one of each, to bask
in its skittish light, I have been parts
of collections and so have you maybe
you will know when you deviate
sure enough what you get
or stop getting until one
day you are standing alone
a blade in the doorway
showering salt into a ripe tomato
it will be late afternoon
a rectangle of sun will stop and rest
a bird will go over
its shade will splash the yard
and the handmaidens industrious
dwelling in every sudden corridor of the workplace
and the mind
and in the paranoid algorithmic tunnels
and in whoever's blood you are snorting
will pause their addled manias
and join you to every melting glacier
and you will pull over out
of your ruined castle –
I was only wearing a tube of red
I was shaking like a virgin
when I learned

the heart hurts more in opening
than it does in breaking.

The earth turned with the moon is bright out look.
I missed a call from my uncle's second wife on my
father's side I'll call her back
but it's him
I'm trying to get to
the one who remembers.
Are you sick of me yet? I want to know
the shape of the room
I want to know
its aspect how the light came in
the street sounds and the shelling
I want to know
your crockery and the crash
of fuchsia against the sky
cyan I'm a rootless nothing
I'm an easy oxalis dancing in the sun
is this unspeakable I am multiplying
leave me alone
tell me everything I'm not your nice person
can't also be kind
and silently walk with you in December 2020
along the mansion-choked roads
of Ladbroke Grove studying Grenfell above
the landscaped gardens
Christmas lights strung
among the velvet hedges
heavy black gates
bearing wrought
iron numbers
finely engineered
cars stretching into
the terminal zero
of the setting sun
while six of the households

who survived are still in
temporary accommodation
three years later
the edge of the pit again
dense grey waves
dragging poison salt
along the steel beach
wet sun
yielding
into solvent
pink detached
the luminous tow
what can I tell you but mathematics
speculation, forecasting
I am skilled at not knowing
but seeing
into the void on a good day is big truth
the future
I looked back
carefully at the tower
and at everything that had happened
and I could not hear
one petal shyly patting
to the ground
without hearing them all drop
what can I tell you
on some unborn plane
you know the magnitude
of what is happening
and of what was happening
all those years ago
I cannot divulge more.
This is no confession
but an attempt to transcribe in one day

my thoughts upon that day
how they travel
through and tell me
there is no secret place
where I am kept
or where I do or do not come from
does not forge my fate
I come from under water
and a place they can't erase
our memory's always stronger than their force
I am the beasts
I root for
will always elude me
their death
is my death too.

We said we'd stop at 10 it's 8.32
and I'm opening the window
my temples are icy
why aren't I unbathed and kissing
in a cold and kind of midnight
blue that crazed and mellow softening
no words will do for or probably
I'm not old enough to write about all that
yet without making it just horny
or bitter or religious
or maybe I haven't known it yet
let's go sit in the shade
nobody owns the shade or did I miss it
outside Tate Britain eating sandwiches by the river
an occasional ginger beer with you
is all I need
but then I thought I needed some other shit
I have no need of I sense an ocean
wave and fortune
drag and swell
something happens then unhappens
leaves a hair outside the braid
young scum my raving little fungus
I know you felt it too
oh stubborn worm I am for you with no worship
there is no tenderness in hustling
for cash outside the rubble factory
to re-rebuild a home
inside a pen between a toxic sea
and wall
a trap within a trap within a trap
and still no shelter
still no light still no water
I am learning my own language

letters of the moon and sun
crest and crescent, arrow
I will find you
I will know you in this life
have you not seen the F-16s burning
through the southern sky
oh my sweet dead friend
I miss you every day.
The night is black-red starless
the lights of Kent roll orange
the estate's Christmas windows blink royal blue
and white, red and green and pink, two days ago
Zionist airstrikes hit a paediatric hospital
a centre for disability services
and several homes in Gaza
soon Mohamed Bouazizi will have been dead for a decade
last week Trump pardoned
the four Blackwater security guards
who opened fire with machine guns, grenades
and snipers onto a crowd of people
in Nisour Square, Baghdad
murdering 12 adults and two children in 2007
please, texts my dad, don't send more news
about our part of the world anymore
I write a heavy note
must we always measure time through death
I laugh at it later with my baby
spiders on my thighs.
I'm sorry. I have no one to talk to
about this so I'm writing
to enter the world
I'm writing to try to stay in it
with you forgive me
I am not sorry.

Acknowledgements

Earlier versions of some of these poems have been published in *Amberflora, The Chicago Review, Ludd Gang, Erotoplasty, Dardashi, Tentacular, Social Text Journal* and *No Matter Mail Matter, 2021*. Thank you to the editors of these publications.

The first epigraph is from Gillian Rose's *Love's Work* (USA: NYRB Classics, 2011). The Bertolt Brecht quote is from his poem 'To Those Born Later' (1940). The last quote is from Adania Shibli's novel *Minor Detail* (trans. Elisabeth Jaquette), UK: Fitzcarraldo Editions, 2020.

Notes

Minnows

The phrase about Europe's indefensibility comes from Aimé Césaire's 1950 essay 'Discourse on Colonialism'.

The phrase 'the palm at the end of my mind' is a slight variation of Wallace Stevens' line 'The palm at the end of the mind' from his poem 'Of Mere Being' (1971).

The line 'my veins don't end in me' is from Roque Dalton's poem 'Como Tú / Like You', (trans. Jack Hirschman).

Sleeping With The Window Open

'I know too much has been made of origins' is Dionne Brand's 'Too much has been made of origins' in *A Map to the Door of No Return: Notes to Belonging* (Canada: Vintage Books, 2002).

My line 'how else to know what names us' is thinking with Fran Lock's 'To name is to own, not / to know' from her poem 'On Weekends' in *Contains Mild Peril* (UK: Out-Spoken Press, 2019).

When writing 'as though the gases the solids / began or ended in you' I was thinking again of Roque Dalton's poem 'Como Tú / Like You', (trans. Jack Hirschman).

'but you needn't kill the maggots to save the festering dog' is a response to Maitreyabandhu's poem 'Asaṅga' in *Yarn* (UK: Bloodaxe, 2015).

I was often thinking of 'Tai: A Yom Kippur Sermon' by Aurora Levins Morales, (web, 2017) while writing this poem, particularly towards the end. The final line is Morales' 'there is nothing to defend'.

Poem (29 December 2020)

'I am here to study what studies' is a response to T.E. Lawrence's 'The beginning and ending of the secret of handling Arabs, is unremitting study of them.' Quoted in Joseph Massad's *Colonial Effects: The Making of National Identity in Jordan*, (USA: Columbia University Press, 2001).

'a fugitive rose' is from 'Odes' by Ricardo Reis (Fernando Pessoa) (translated by Edouard Roditi), 'I love / Most of all those fugitive roses / That on the day they are born, / That very day, must also die'.

'Minor details' is another reference to Shibli's novel (see above).

I must have been thinking of Adrienne Rich's poem 'Diving into the Wreck' (1973) when I wrote 'the cool depth of the wreck' and 'diving out of paradise'.

'pinhole image shows an almost / infinite depth of field / where everything's in focus' is from the Wikipedia page for 'Pinhole Camera'. Ibn al-Haytham (965–1039), the Muslim Arab mathematician, astronomer and physicist of the Islamic Golden Age, was one of the first to describe the effects of the camera obscura; as well as key facts about light and perception. Scholars have argued that al-Haytham should be credited with many discoveries and theories previously attributed to western Europeans writing centuries later. It was him I was thinking of when I wrote the words 'a theory of light' earlier in this poem.

When I wrote 'I know who decides whose violence is violent' I was thinking of Kwame Ture's essay 'The Pitfalls of Liberalism' (1969) where he writes, 'The oppressor is only opposed to violence when the oppressed talk about using violence against the oppressor.'

'Bernadette writes of chopping a carrot / how it seems to be returning to itself as seed' is a direct reference to Mayer's *Midwinter Day*, 'I love chopping vegetables where you do something to make something that is one idiosyncratic thing into many things all looking the same or identical, much like the vegetables' original seeds.'

The Emily I am referring to in 'like when Emily writes' is Emily Brontë. The quote about dreams which follows is from her 1847 novel *Wuthering Heights*.

The Audre I refer to is Audre Lorde. The section from 'white margarine' to 'bursts into me too' is a reference to her essay 'Uses of the Erotic: The Erotic as Power' (UK: Silver Press, 2017) where she writes:

'During World War II, we bought sealed plastic packets of white, uncolored margarine, with a tiny, intense pellet of yellow coloring perched like a topaz just inside the clear skin of the bag. We would leave the margarine out for a while to soften, and then we would pinch the little pellet to break it inside the bag, releasing the rich yellowness into the soft pale mass of margarine. Then taking it carefully between our fingers, we would knead it gently back and forth, over and over, until the color had spread throughout the whole pound bag of margarine, thoroughly coloring it.

I find the erotic such a kernel within myself. When released from its intense and constrained pellet, it flows through and colors my life with a kind of energy that heightens and sensitizes and strengthens all my experience.'

'a dying tree / a young woman / recognises the folly of withdrawal' is both a reference to Alicia Ostriker's poem 'A Young Woman, A Tree' (1987) and a direct quote, 'Recognizes the folly of desire, / The folly of withdrawal'.

'six of the households / who survived are still in / temporary accommodation / three years later'. I got this figure from The Royal Borough of Kensington and Chelsea's website in December 2020 at the time of writing. At the time of editing, June 2021 (almost four years to the day since the fire), the figure remains the same.

'This is no confession / but an attempt to transcribe in one day / my thoughts upon that day' is another direct reference to *Midwinter Day* where Mayer writes, 'I had an idea to write a book that would translate the detail of thought from a day to language like a dream transformed to read as it does, everything, a book that would end before it started in time to prove the day like the dream has everything in it, to do this without remembering like a dream inciting writing continuously for as long as you can stand up till you fall down like in a story to show and possess everything we know because having it all at once is performing a magical service for survival by the use of the mind like memory.'

'let's go sit in the shade / nobody owns the shade' is my translation (from the Arabic) of a lyric from the first song, 'بلا ولا شي / Bala Wala Chi (Without Anything)', on Ziad Al Rahbani's wonderful album هدوء نسبي / *Houdou Nisbi (Relative Calm)* (1984).

Four security guards from the private military firm Blackwater (renamed Xe Services in 2009, re-renamed Academi in 2011) 'were part of an armoured convoy that opened fire indiscriminately with machine-guns, grenade launchers and a sniper on a crowd of unarmed people in [Nisour] square in [Baghdad]' killing 14 civilians on 16 September 2007. The names of the guards are Paul Slough, Evan Liberty, Dustin Heard and Nicholas Slatten. Slattern was sentenced to life and the others to 30 years in prison each. On Wednesday 23 December 2020 they were pardoned by Donald Trump. The names of the 14 murdered people are Ahmed Haithem Ahmed Al Rubia'y, Mahassin Mohssen

Kadhum Al-Khazali, Osama Fadhil Abbas, Ali Mohammed Hafedh Abdul Razzaq, Mohamed Abbas Mahmoud, Qasim Mohamed Abbas Mahmoud, Sa'adi Ali Abbas Alkarkh, Mushtaq Karim Abd Al-Razzaq, Ghaniyah Hassan Ali, Ibrahim Abid Ayash, Hamoud Sa'eed Abttan, Uday Ismail Ibrahiem, Mahdi Sahib Nasir and Ali Khalil Abdul Hussein (information and quote from *The Guardian*).

Thanks

This collection would not have happened without Cai and Ellen who were the first readers of much earlier versions of 'Minnows', back in the Spring of 2020 when we were writing to and with each other regularly and in emergency. Thank you.

My gratitude to Pauline for sharing her artworks with me and collaborating on the cover, and for her feedback and support while I was making this work.

Thank you to Lotte for her generous and detailed feedback on this collection.

Thank you to Azad and Kashif for their feedback, support and patience, and to the87press team for making this book happen.

For their capacity to imagine other possible worlds and still love this one, and for their constance and friendship I thank Jen, Lidija, Julia, Pauline, Phoebe, Dierdre, Lotte, Emilia, Sarona, Ellie, Darsavini, John and Mike.

And with utmost gratitude and love to my family and to my south London family. Without you I have nothing.